FINANCIAL
ABUNDANCE
for
CHILDREN

FINANCIAL ABUNDANCE —for— CHILDREN

VIKAS ARORA

Worldwide Published by

Pendown Press

PENDOWN PRESS LLP
An ISO 9001 & ISO 14001 Certified Co.,
Regd. Office: 3767A, Kanhaiya Nagar,
Tri Nagar, Delhi-110035
Ph.: 8130886000, 9650072927
E-mail: info@pendownpress.com
Branch Office: 1A/2A, 20, Hari Sadan, Ansari Road,
Daryaganj, New Delhi-110002
Ph.: 011-45794768
Website: PendownPress.com

Edition: 2024
Price: ₹ 259/-
ISBN: 978-93-6338-595-5

Layout and Cover Designed by Pendown Graphics Team
Printed and Bound in India by Thomson Press India Ltd.

DEDICATION

CONTENTS

❖ ❖ ❖ ❖

ACKNOWLEDGEMENTS

I extend my heartfelt gratitude to the numerous individuals who have played a pivotal role in bringing this book to fruition. Their unwavering support, insightful discussions, constructive feedback, and assistance in editing, proofreading, and design have been invaluable to this project's success.

Foremost, I express my deepest appreciation to my parents, whose constant love and guidance have been an unwavering source of strength throughout this endeavour. They are my ultimate role models, and I am profoundly grateful for their encouragement.

I would like to extend special thanks to my mentor, Sh. R. Gopinath, the Managing Director of M/s Gopast Centre for Learning Pvt. Ltd., Chennai. His profound teachings on various concepts have been instrumental in reaching the milestones of this journey. I am humbled by his blessings and eager to continue learning from him.

My heartfelt thanks go to my loving and supportive wife, Priyal, and my two wonderful children, Daksh and Saanvi. Their unyielding encouragement and inspiration have been an anchor in my pursuit of this project.

Lastly, I sincerely apologize to all those who have been a part of my 25-year journey and whose names might have inadvertently been omitted in this acknowledgment. Your contributions have been deeply valued and appreciated.

Thank you all for being an integral part of this remarkable journey.

❖ ❖ ❖ ❖

PREFACE

In God's creations, when we compare animals and birds with humans, one thing is prevalent: they love their children just as we do.

However, what differentiates us from them is our sense of duties and responsibilities.

As parents, I am certain all of you will agree that one of our major duties is ensuring our children's future needs are met in abundance.

This encompasses planning for their education, career, marriage, and even business ventures by choosing **the best methods of, risk-free investments yielding abundant returns to ensure availability of funds when needed.**

Creating a need and time-based investment portfolio ensures that you never have to worry or struggle to provide the best for your child at the cost of your health and mental peace.

Unfortunately, in our industry, many people mis-sell products under the guise of child insurance, focusing solely on their benefit. They sell various plans in the name of securing a child's future without considering the actual needs and potential benefits for the child.

It's heartbreaking to see parents being misled into buying inappropriate products that do little to truly secure their child's future.

A true financial planner, however, understands the intricate balance between immediate needs and future aspirations.

They provide the right approach, ensuring that every financial decision made today contributes meaningfully towards a child's long-term goals. The importance of early planning cannot be overstated.

It is not just about having a savings plan but about creating a comprehensive strategy that encompasses all aspects of a child's future – from securing a world-class education to establishing a successful career, ensuring a happy marriage, and potentially setting up a business.

In this book, we will delve into the stories of business families who have successfully planned for their children's futures. These inspiring tales will highlight the practical steps they took and the challenges they overcame.

We will also explore various strategies and financial tools available to parents to help them create an abundance of opportunities for their children.

Each chapter will provide insights and actionable advice on how to navigate the complexities of financial planning for a child's future. By the end of this book, you will be equipped with the knowledge and tools to ensure that your child's dreams can become a reality, free from the financial burdens that often hinder such aspirations. We will discuss in detail how to create abundance for your child's future needs, setting a strong foundation for a prosperous and fulfilling life.

CHAPTER 1

THE DREAM BEGINS

"You have to dream before your dreams can come true."
– A. P. J. Abdul Kalam

The Power of Vision

Every great achievement starts with a dream. Dreams are the seeds from which the future grows, and as parents, envisioning a bright and prosperous future for our children is the first step towards making it a reality. Our dreams for our children are not just about seeing them achieve success but about providing them with the tools and opportunities to carve their paths and realize their full potential as illustrated by two real-world stories shared below.

It All Begins With a Dream!

Visualize the story of Raj and Priya, a couple from a small town who dreamed of their daughter, Aanya, studying at a prestigious university abroad.

Despite their modest means, they were determined to give Aanya the best possible education. They meticulously planned and saved, cutting back on personal luxuries and investing in educational resources.

Raj and Priya's unwavering belief in their dream for Aanya's future was the driving force behind their sacrifices. With the right financial guidance and prudent and timely investments, they did make their dream come true. However, it all started with a vision.

Their story is a testament to the power of vision and the extraordinary lengths parents will go to ensure their children's success.

A Mother's Dedicated Vision Bears Fruit!

Another inspiring tale is that of Meena, a single mother who worked multiple jobs to support her son, Rohit.

Meena dreamed of Rohit becoming a renowned scientist. She filled their small apartment with books and educational toys, fostering an environment of learning and curiosity.

Despite the odds, Meena's relentless dedication and clear vision for Rohit's future paid off when he received a scholarship to a top research university. Her story illustrates how a clear vision, coupled with determination, can transform dreams into reality.

Building a Solid Foundation

While dreams are the starting point, building a solid foundation is crucial for turning those dreams into tangible outcomes. Early childhood education plays a pivotal role in shaping a child's future. The first few years of a child's life are incredibly formative, with the brain developing at an astonishing rate. Providing a stimulating and nurturing environment during these early years sets the stage for lifelong learning and success.

Consider the story of Arun and Suman, who understood the importance of early childhood education for their twins, Aryan and Anaya. They invested in quality preschool programs that emphasized not just academic learning but also social skills, emotional development, and creativity. They encouraged their children to explore, ask questions, and engage in hands-on activities. This holistic approach to early education helped Aryan and Anaya develop a love for learning, which stayed with them as they grew older.

Cultivating curiosity and a love for learning in young minds is one of the greatest gifts parents can give their children. It's not just about academic success; it's about nurturing a lifelong passion for discovery and growth. When children are encouraged to be curious and explore the world around them, they develop critical thinking skills and a sense of wonder that drives them to seek knowledge and solutions throughout their lives.

Take the example of Jatin and Rina, who encouraged their son, Karan, to pursue his interests from a young age. Whether it was building elaborate Lego structures, conducting simple science experiments at home, or reading about distant galaxies, they supported and celebrated his curiosity. Karan's early experiences with exploring his interests laid the foundation for his future success as an engineer, showcasing how a love for learning, instilled early on, can lead to remarkable achievements.

In conclusion, the dream for our children's future begins with a vision.

It's the dream that ignites our efforts and sets us on a path of dedication and planning. By building a solid foundation through early childhood education and fostering a love for learning, we provide our children with the essential tools to turn those dreams into reality. The stories of Raj and Priya, Meena, Arun and Suman, and Jatin and Rina highlight the profound impact of vision, early education, and nurturing curiosity on a child's journey to success.

As we move forward in this book, we will explore more strategies and insights to help you create abundance and opportunity for your child's future, ensuring that your dreams for them are not just wishes but achievable goals.

CHAPTER 2

UNDERSTANDING & NURTURING YOUR CHILD'S UNIQUE TALENTS

"If we nurture the dreams of children, the world will be blessed. If we destroy them, the world is doomed!"
- Wes Stafford

Every child is born with unique talents and interests. As parents, one of our most important jobs is to help identify these natural abilities and passions early on. This is not just about recognizing academic strengths but also about seeing where their hearts truly lie. Whether it's a knack for drawing, a love for music, a fascination with numbers, or an interest in sports, these are the seeds of their future success.

An Artist is Nurtured Not Born!

Take the story of Anil and Sunita, who noticed that their daughter, Kavya, loved to paint. Instead of brushing it off as a mere hobby, they encouraged her by providing her with painting supplies and enrolling her in art classes. They didn't pressure her to excel but simply gave her the tools and space to explore her interests. Over time, Kavya's passion for painting grew, leading her to win several art competitions and eventually pursue a career as a professional artist.

Encouraging your child's natural abilities also means providing them with diverse opportunities to explore different fields. Sometimes, children need to try a variety of activities before they find what truly excites them. This exploration phase is crucial because it allows them to discover their strengths and interests in a supportive environment.

It's equally important to consider the cultural context when nurturing your child's talents. For example, if your family has a tradition of classical music, exposing your child to this art form can be a way of connecting them with their heritage while fostering talent. Similarly, traditional dance, craft, or storytelling can be wonderful avenues for children to explore their abilities and stay connected to their cultural roots.

Creating a Supportive Environment

A nurturing and stimulating home atmosphere is essential for a child's development. This means creating a space where they feel safe to express themselves and are encouraged to learn and grow.

A supportive environment is not just about physical space but also about emotional support.

Ramesh and Aarti made sure their home was filled with books, educational toys, and creative materials. They set up a small corner where their children could read, draw, and play. More importantly, they spent time with their children, engaging in activities together, and showing genuine interest in their pursuits. This not only nurtured their children's talents but also built a strong family bond.

The role of family and community in a child's development cannot be overstated. Children learn a great deal from their immediate environment, and the values and traditions they see around them play a significant role in shaping their character. By involving family members in a child's learning journey, parents can reinforce positive values and provide a broader support system.

For instance, Meera's grandparents played a big part in her upbringing. They shared stories from their past, taught her traditional crafts, and involved her in community activities. This not only gave Meera a sense of belonging but also helped her appreciate her cultural heritage. It taught her the importance of family and community, values that stayed with her as she grew up.

Creating a supportive environment also means encouraging children to take risks and learn from their failures.

Instead of shielding them from challenges, parents can teach them to see mistakes as opportunities to learn and grow. This resilience will serve them well in all aspects of life.

In conclusion, planting the seeds of future success involves nurturing your child's talents and interests and creating a supportive environment for their growth. By identifying their natural abilities, providing diverse opportunities for exploration, and involving family and community in their development, parents can help children build a strong foundation for their future. The stories of Anil and Sunita, Ramesh and Aarti, and Meera's grandparents highlight the importance of these practices. As we move forward, we will explore more ways to support our children's journeys, ensuring they have the resources and encouragement they need to thrive.

CHAPTER 3

EXPLORING & PREPPING FOR WORLD-CLASS EDUCATION

> *"A child without education is like a*
> *bird without wings."*
> *— Tibetan Proverb*

Every parent dreams of giving their child the best education possible. But with so many options out there, it can be overwhelming to decide what's best for your child. The key is to start exploring educational opportunities early on.

This means looking at both local and international schools, understanding their programs, and seeing which ones align with your child's interests and strengths.

For example, Rohan and Priya wanted their son, Aditya, to have a world-class education. They started by researching top schools and universities around the world. They looked into the programs offered, the admission requirements, and the overall reputation of these institutions. They also considered schools that focused on Aditya's interests, such as science and technology. By doing this research early, they were able to plan better and set realistic goals for Aditya's education.

A Lifetime of Guilt: A Tale of Lost Opportunities

While it is our love-fueled duty and responsibility to nurture our children's talents and provide a supportive and conducive environment, we also must be financially ready to give them the best when the time comes for education and higher studies.

There are times when, despite our best efforts, certain educational opportunities may be out of reach.

It's a difficult moment when your child can't pursue higher studies due to lack of availability or financial constraints. These situations can be disheartening, but they also highlight the importance of early planning and setting clear priorities.

A Tale of Broken Dreams....

Take the story of Anjali and Manoj, whose daughter, Pooja, dreamt of studying medicine abroad and they were supportive of her in every way. However, when the moment of decision came, the costs were astronomical, and they couldn't afford it at the last minute.

This was a heartbreaking time for the family, all of Pooja's dreams were shattered.

The parents were overwhelmed with guilt at having failed their child.

However, this guilt moment made them realize the importance of starting early with a financial plan that could support such dreams. It was a hard lesson, but it pushed them to be more proactive for their younger son's future.

Financial Planning for Education: Giving Wings to Dreams

Planning for your child's education is not just about saving money; it's about having a comprehensive financial strategy.

This means prioritizing your financial goals to ensure that essential needs are met without compromising on significant future goals.

Early identification of these priorities helps avoid the pitfalls of spending on a first-come, first-serve basis and the need for high-interest loans.

For instance, Suresh and Kavita made a financial plan as soon as their daughter, Meera, was born. They set up an education savings account and contributed to it regularly. They also looked into scholarships and grants that Meera could apply for in the future.

This early planning gave them peace of mind and ensured that Meera would have the funds she needed to pursue her dreams without financial stress.

Leveraging Scholarships, Grants, and Financial Aid

One of the smartest ways to manage the cost of education is to explore scholarships, grants, and financial aid. These are funds that don't need to be repaid and can significantly reduce the financial burden. Many institutions offer scholarships based on academic merit, sports achievements, or even specific talents.

Rekha and Arjun encouraged their son, Kunal, to apply for various scholarships as he prepared for college. They found that many universities offered financial aid packages that covered a significant portion of the tuition fees. By staying informed and proactive, they were able to secure the financial assistance Kunal needed, making higher education more affordable.

Prioritizing Financial Goals

It's important to prioritize financial goals to ensure that all essential needs are met.

This means having a clear understanding of your financial situation and making informed decisions about spending and saving.

By doing this, you can avoid unnecessary expenses and focus on what truly matters for your child's future.

Jyoti and Mahesh decided to manage & optimize their spending to support their son, Arnav's, education. They cut down on luxury expenses and redirected those funds into an education savings plan. They also created a detailed budget to track their expenses and savings. This disciplined approach helped them stay on track and ensured that they had enough funds to support Arnav's educational aspirations.

In conclusion, preparing for a world-class education involves exploring various educational opportunities, planning for potential challenges, and having a solid financial strategy.

By starting early, prioritizing financial goals, and seeking out scholarships and grants, parents can ensure that their children have the resources they need to achieve their dreams. The stories of Rohan and Priya, Anjali and Manoj, Suresh and Kavita, Rekha and Arjun, and Jyoti and Mahesh illustrate the importance of these practices. As we continue, we will explore more strategies to support your child's educational journey, ensuring a bright and successful future.

CHAPTER 4

OVERCOMING FINANCIAL HURDLES

"Our goals can only be reached through a vehicle of a plan, in which we must fervently believe, and upon which we must vigorously act. There is no other route to success."
— Pablo Picasso

Children Working to Pay for Education

One of the harsh realities many families face is the need for children to work while they study to cover their college fees. This situation is particularly common for those studying abroad, where tuition and living costs can be exorbitant. While working can teach valuable life skills, it often comes at the cost of academic performance and personal well-being.

Walking The Tight Rope:
The Challenge of Balancing Study & Work

Take the story of Rohit, a bright student who got accepted into a prestigious university in the United States. Despite securing partial scholarships, the financial gap was too large for his family to cover entirely.

To make ends meet, Rohit took up multiple part-time jobs. Balancing work and study proved to be incredibly challenging. His grades began to suffer, and the stress took a toll on his health.

While he managed to graduate, the journey was far from ideal.

His story highlights the importance of adequate financial planning to prevent children from bearing such burdens.

The Burden on Parents

Often, the financial strain of higher education falls on parents, who end up paying off education loans from their limited pensions. This scenario is all too familiar in many households where parents prioritize their children's education above their own financial security. The emotional and financial toll can be overwhelming.

A Debt & Anxiety Ridden Retirement!

Consider the case of Rajesh and Meera, who took out substantial loans to fund their daughter, Aisha's, medical education.

As they retired, a significant portion of their pension went towards repaying these loans.

The financial strain left them with little for their own needs, causing stress and anxiety.

This situation underscores the necessity of a comprehensive financial strategy that safeguards both the child's and the parents' futures.

Ensuring a Debt-Free Start for Young Professionals

Starting a career burdened by education loans is a common predicament for many young professionals.

This financial pressure can hinder their ability to save, invest, and achieve financial independence.

Therefore, it's crucial to implement strategies that prevent this scenario.

Ravi, a young engineer, began his career with a hefty student loan hanging over his head. His early salary went primarily towards loan repayments, leaving little for savings or personal expenses.

To avoid such situations, families must plan early and consider various funding options like scholarships, grants, and education savings plans.

Ensuring that young professionals start their careers debt-free allows them to build a solid financial foundation for their future.

Financial Needs: Ongoing & Major Responsibilities and Uncertainties

Financial planning for a family involves addressing both ongoing needs and major responsibilities. Ongoing needs include daily expenses like food, clothes, school fees, and utility bills, requiring a steady cash flow. Major responsibilities, on the other hand, require lump-sum amounts for significant life events like higher education, marriage, or buying a home.

For instance, Suman and Deepak carefully mapped out their financial responsibilities. They maintained a detailed budget for their ongoing needs and set up separate savings for major milestones like their children's college education and weddings. This approach ensured that they could meet their daily expenses without compromising on long-term goals.

Life is unpredictable, and planning for uncertainties is an integral part of financial planning. The death of the primary earning member can derail a family's financial goals. To mitigate such risks, having adequate life insurance and a contingency plan is essential.

A Grief-Stricken Household Saved From Uncertainty

Anjali's husband, Vikram, was the main breadwinner.

When he unexpectedly passed away, Anjali found herself in a financial crisis.

Fortunately, Vikram had a comprehensive life insurance policy, which provided financial support during this difficult time.

This example illustrates the importance of preparing for unforeseen events to protect the family's financial future.

In conclusion, overcoming financial hurdles requires thorough planning and strategic financial management. By addressing the need for children to work while studying, alleviating the financial burden on parents, ensuring young professionals start their careers debt-free, managing ongoing and major financial responsibilities, and preparing for uncertainties, families can navigate financial challenges more effectively.

The stories of Rohit, Rajesh and Meera, Ravi, Suman and Deepak, and Anjali highlight these critical aspects of financial planning. As we move forward, we will explore more strategies to ensure financial security and success for your family.

CHAPTER 5

Creating Financial Provisions – Making Marriage Joyful Not Stressful

"The most beautiful weddings are those where love, laughter, and joy take center stage, leaving stress behind."
– Vikas Arora

In Indian culture, every parent dreams of an auspicious and grand marriage for their son or daughter.

This cherished tradition symbolizes not just the union of two individuals but the coming together of two families.

However, the cost of hosting such a wedding is sharply rising due to changing trends, fashion, choices, and aspirations.

The growing expenses can put significant financial pressure on families, making it essential to plan well in advance.

The Rising Costs of Grand Marriages

The traditional Indian wedding has always been an elaborate affair, but today's weddings often feature even more lavish elements. From designer outfits and destination venues to high-end catering and elaborate decorations, the expenses can quickly add up.

Parents often feel the pressure to meet these expectations, ensuring that their child's wedding is memorable and prestigious. However, without proper financial planning, these costs can become overwhelming.

Amit and Priya, who wanted their daughter, Nisha, to have a wedding that everyone would remember, handled the situation brilliantly. They started by creating a detailed budget, considering all aspects of the event. From the engagement ceremony to the reception, they outlined every expense. By doing so, they could prioritize their spending and ensure they were prepared for the big day without financial strain.

The Importance of Early Financial Planning

Early financial planning is crucial to managing the costs of a grand wedding. By starting to save early, parents can accumulate the necessary funds over time, reducing the need for loans or last-minute financial scrambles.

Creating a dedicated wedding fund can be an effective strategy. This fund can grow through regular contributions and smart investments, ensuring that the money is available when needed.

A Wedding To Remember Minus Financial Strain

Take the example of Rajesh and Meera, who started a wedding fund as soon as their son, Arjun, was born. They made small, consistent contributions and invested the money in safe, long-term instruments. By the time Arjun was ready to get married, the fund had grown significantly, covering most of the wedding expenses. This proactive approach ensured that Rajesh and Meera could provide a beautiful wedding for their son without compromising their financial stability.

Sacrificing Aspirations for Reality

While it's natural to want the best for your child's wedding, **aligning grand aspirations with financial reality is essential.** This often means making thoughtful compromises to stay within budget. Open communication with your child about financial limits and priorities can help manage expectations and focus on meaningful aspects of the wedding.

Consider the story of Anil and Sunita's daughter, Kavya. When she got engaged, Kavya dreamt of a destination wedding in an exotic location. However, after sitting down as a family to discuss the financial implications, they realized that such a wedding was beyond their budget.

Leveraging Financial Tools

There are several financial tools available to help plan and save for a wedding. Fixed deposits, mutual funds, and recurring deposit accounts can provide steady growth over time. **Additionally, insurance plans specifically designed for wedding expenses can offer security and peace of mind.**

When Vinay and Rekha were planning their daughter's wedding, they opted for a combination of investments. They used mutual funds for long-term growth and fixed deposits for stability. This diversified approach helped them build a substantial wedding fund that could handle both expected and unexpected expenses.

Avoiding the Pitfall of Debt

One of the key goals of financial planning for a wedding should be to avoid debt. While loans might seem like an easy solution, they can lead to financial stress and strain relationships. By planning ahead and saving diligently, families can ensure that they do not have to rely on borrowing to finance the wedding.

Priya and Sanjay chose to save methodically for their son's wedding. Despite the temptation to take out a loan for additional extravagance, they stuck to their budget. The wedding was beautiful and well within their means, allowing them to enjoy the celebration without the shadow of debt.

In conclusion, creating a provision for an auspicious marriage requires foresight, planning, and disciplined saving. The rising costs of grand weddings in Indian culture make it imperative for parents to start financial planning early. By understanding the expenses, leveraging financial tools, balancing aspirations with reality, and avoiding debt, families can ensure that their child's wedding is a joyous and memorable occasion without financial strain.

As we move forward, we will explore more strategies to ensure financial security and success for your family.

CHAPTER 6

Creating a Financial Provision for Your Child's Business

"Financial planning is the silent partner in every successful venture, turning dreams into achievable goals and ensuring growth is sustainable."
– Vikas Arora

The Importance of Financial Planning for Business Ventures

In today's competitive world, setting up a business can be a powerful way to ensure your child's future success. Many parents dream of providing a solid foundation for their children by helping them start their own business. This could mean setting up a new factory, launching a new product line, or starting a new vertical within an existing business. Proper financial planning is crucial to make this dream a reality.

Starting a business from scratch requires significant financial investment, strategic planning, and a strong support system. Consider the story of Mr. Sharma, who always dreamed of setting up a factory for his son, Rohit. Mr. Sharma understood that merely having the capital was not enough; careful planning and financial provisioning were essential.

He began by creating a detailed financial plan that included market research, cost estimates, and a timeline for the business launch. He also set up a separate fund dedicated to this project, ensuring that the necessary capital was available when needed. This proactive approach allowed Rohit to start his factory smoothly, with all the financial backing required to handle initial costs and unforeseen expenses.

Encouraging the Entrepreneurial Spirit

Encouraging your child to develop an entrepreneurial mindset is key. This means nurturing their interests, providing them with the necessary resources, and helping them understand the importance of financial management.

A Launch Built Up Over the years....

Early on in her childhood, Priya's parents noticed her talent for fashion design. They encouraged her to develop this talent by enrolling her in design courses and also exposing her to the business side of fashion.

Additionally, Priya's parents also set up a financial corpus to support her dream of launching her own fashion line.

With a solid financial foundation and her parents' guidance, Priya successfully started her own clothing brand going on to do very well.

Creating a Financial Corpus

Creating a financial corpus involves setting aside funds specifically for your child's business ventures. This fund should be built gradually over time through disciplined saving and smart investments.

Ravi and Meera wanted to ensure their son, Arjun, could start his own tech company after graduating. They began saving early, investing in mutual funds and other high-growth assets to build a substantial corpus. By the time Arjun was ready to launch his business, the financial support was in place, allowing him to focus on innovation and growth without worrying about initial funding.

In many family-run businesses, leveraging existing resources can provide a significant advantage. Expanding an existing business or starting a new vertical can be more manageable with the support and infrastructure already in place.

Mr. Patel's Foresight Launches Aisha's Success

For instance, Mr. Patel, who owned a successful manufacturing business, wanted to help his daughter, Aisha, start a new product line.

By utilizing the existing factory space, machinery, and supply chain, Aisha could launch her new venture with lower initial costs.

Mr. Patel also set up a financial corpus specifically for this expansion, ensuring that Aisha had the capital needed to innovate and grow.

Navigating Financial Challenges

Every business faces financial challenges, whether it's managing cash flow, handling unexpected expenses, or dealing with market fluctuations. Preparing your child to navigate these challenges is crucial for long-term success.

Deepak and Shweta helped their son, Rohan, start a food processing business. Despite careful planning, the business faced initial setbacks due to market competition.

However, because they had set aside a contingency fund as part of their financial planning, Rohan could weather the storm and eventually find success.

This experience underscored the importance of not only providing financial support but also planning for uncertainties.

Creating a financial provision for your child's business is an investment in their future. By building a financial corpus, encouraging entrepreneurial thinking, leveraging family resources, and preparing for financial challenges, you can provide a solid foundation for your child's business ventures.

CHAPTER 7

INTEGRATED LIFE PLANNING

"Personal finance is only 20% head knowledge.
It's 80% behaviour!"
– Dave Ramsey

In today's fast-paced world, planning for your child's future is more important than ever. Financial planning ensures that your child has the resources they need to pursue their dreams, whether it's for education, starting a business, or securing their future.

By integrating life planning with financial strategies, you can create a solid foundation for your child's success.

Here are some key features of integrating financial planning into your daily life and making it a way of life, rather than being something that you do as and when randomly.

➢ **Balancing Personal and Professional Life**

Balancing personal and professional life is crucial for both parents and children. When parents manage their time effectively, they can provide better support and guidance for their children. This balance helps create a stable environment where children can thrive.

Consider the story of Ramesh and Sita, who both worked full-time jobs while raising their two children. They made it a priority to spend quality time with their kids, helping with homework, attending school events, and having family dinners. This balance ensured that their children felt supported and valued, while Ramesh and Sita managed their careers effectively.

➤ The Importance of Early Financial Planning

Early financial planning can make a significant difference in your child's future. **Starting early allows you to save money over a longer period, increasing the potential for growth.** This planning can cover various aspects, from education to starting a business or even ensuring a comfortable retirement for your child.

Deepak and Meera started an education savings plan for their daughter, Priya, as soon as she was born. They made regular contributions, which grew over time. By the time Priya was ready for college, they had enough funds to cover her tuition and other expenses, allowing her to focus on her studies without financial stress.

➤ Creating a Financial Corpus

As discussed in the previous chapter setting aside funds to create a financial corpus specifically for your child's future needs is extremely important. This fund can be built gradually through disciplined saving and wise financial decisions. The goal is to accumulate enough resources to support significant life events, such as higher education, starting a business, or purchasing a home.

➤ Planning for Unexpected Events

Life is unpredictable, and planning for unexpected events is a critical part of financial planning. This means having insurance coverage, an emergency fund, and a contingency plan to handle unforeseen circumstances.

Raj and Priya ensured they had adequate life and health insurance coverage. When Raj unexpectedly fell ill, the insurance provided the financial support needed to cover medical expenses and maintain their lifestyle. This planning allowed Priya and their children to focus on Raj's recovery without the added stress of financial worries.

➤ **Leaving a Legacy**

Planning for your child's future also involves thinking about the legacy you want to leave behind. **This includes financial assets and the values, traditions, and life lessons that will guide your children throughout their lives.**

Anand and Preeti made it a point to involve their children in family discussions about finances, teaching them the importance of saving, making smart financial choices, and giving back to the community. They also created a will and set up trusts to ensure their assets were distributed according to their wishes. By planning their legacy, Anand and Preeti provided their children with a clear understanding of their family's values and the resources to uphold them.

➤ **Comprehensive Financial Strategies**

To secure your child's future, it's essential to have a comprehensive financial strategy. This involves budgeting for daily expenses, saving for future needs, and making wise financial decisions to grow your wealth. It also means considering your child's education, potential business ventures, and even their future families.

When Rohit and Kavita's daughter, Aisha, was born, they immediately started an education savings plan. They also set aside funds for Aisha's potential business ventures and her future wedding. By planning comprehensively, they ensured that they could support Aisha through various stages of her life without financial strain.

> **Budgeting for Daily Expenses**

Managing daily expenses is a crucial part of a strategic financial plan. By creating and sticking to a budget, you can ensure that you're living within your means and saving for the future. A budget helps you track where your money is going and make adjustments as needed.

For example, Neha and Rajesh created a monthly budget to manage their household expenses. They tracked their spending on groceries, utilities, and other necessities, and made sure to set aside a portion of their income for savings. This disciplined approach helped them save money over time, which they used to support their children's education and other needs.

> **Saving for Future Needs**

In addition to managing daily expenses, it's important to save for future needs. This could include anything from your child's college education to their first car or even their wedding. Setting specific financial goals and saving towards them can help you stay focused and motivated.

Sunil and Meera wanted to ensure they had enough money to pay for their daughter, Rhea's, higher education. They calculated the estimated costs and set a monthly savings goal. By consistently saving a small amount each month, they were able to accumulate a significant fund by the time Rhea finished high school.

> **Making Wise Financial Decisions**

Making wise financial decisions involves choosing the right

savings options and avoiding unnecessary expenses. This might include choosing a savings account with a good interest rate, avoiding high-interest loans, and being mindful of your spending habits.

For instance, Kavita and Arjun decided to avoid taking out a loan for their son's college fees. Instead, they focused on saving and investing their money wisely over the years. This careful planning ensured that they had enough funds to pay for their son's education without going into debt.

Integrated life planning is about creating a balanced and secure environment for your child's future. By balancing personal and professional life, pursuing continuous personal growth, planning for unexpected events, leaving a meaningful legacy, and implementing comprehensive financial strategies, you can ensure your child's success.

CHAPTER 8

COMMON OBJECTIONS AND THE CONSEQUENCES OF LATE PLANNING

A year from now you may wish you had started today."
– Karen Lamb

The importance of early financial planning cannot be emphasized enough, by now I am sure you understand it well enough, yet let me tell you that Many parents have various objections when it comes to planning for their child's future.

Common Objections to Planning for the Child's Future

Let's address these common objections point by point:

1. **"Aaj ki priorities kuch aur hai" (Today's priorities are different)**

   It's essential to recognize that while current priorities are important, setting aside even a small amount regularly can make a significant difference in the long run. Future needs should not be neglected.

2. **"Abhi mujhe business grow karna hai, that needs a good amount of money" (I need to grow my business, which requires a lot of money)**

Balancing business investments and saving for your child's future can be challenging, but it's possible. Allocating a small percentage of your income towards your child's future can provide financial security without compromising business growth.

3. **"Abhi ghar or car ki EMI bhi deni hai every month" (I have to pay home and car EMIs every month)**

While EMIs are a fixed expense, budgeting wisely can help you manage both your loans and your savings for your child's future. Consider refinancing options or cutting down on non-essential expenses to free up funds.

4. **"Business down hai, payments nahi aa rahi hai logo se" (Business is down, payments are not coming in from clients)**

Financial setbacks are part of life. During such times, it's crucial to adjust your savings strategy. Even small contributions during tough times can accumulate over time.

5. **"Abhi bahut time hai child education mein, why to worry now" (There's still a lot of time before my child needs higher education, so why worry now)?**

Starting early gives you the advantage of compounding, allowing your savings to grow significantly over time. Delaying savings can result in financial strain later.

6. **"It's a long commitment, maybe I will not be able to afford"**

Financial planning is about setting realistic goals and adjusting them as circumstances change. A flexible plan can accommodate changes in your financial situation.

7. **"Future acha karne ke liye aaj present bhi to nahi kharab karna" (To secure the future, we should not spoil the present)**

   Striking a balance is key. By planning wisely and prioritizing your expenses, you can ensure a comfortable present while securing the future.

Sadly these are just excuses that will only cause stress and heartbreak for both you and your children later on. For such parents, all I can say is that if the benefits of early financial planning couldn't get you into action, let me show you the darker side of the picture.

Let me show you the consequences of late financial planning.

The Consequences of Late Planning

Typically, when kids reach the age of 10-12 years, some parents start thinking about their child's education. However, by this time, it may already be too late to accumulate the necessary funds without financial stress.

Delayed planning often results in the need to take out loans, which come with their own set of challenges.

Parents who delay planning may find themselves paying off education loans well into their retirement.

This situation can strain their finances, as they may end up using their pension to pay off these loans instead of covering their basic and essential needs during old age. Proper financial planning from an early stage can help avoid these pitfalls and ensure that parents and children are financially secure.

The Importance of Accurate Financial Estimation

Some parents start planning early but fail to accurately estimate the amount required for their child's education at the time of university admission.

This miscalculation can result in insufficient funds and the need for bank loans, which adds financial pressure.

To avoid this, parents should regularly review and adjust their financial plans to account for inflation, rising education costs, and changes in their financial situation. Consulting with financial advisors and using education cost calculators can provide a clearer picture of the required savings. This thorough and regular planning ensures that parents are well-prepared for their child's education expenses without financial strain.

CHAPTER 9

THE JOURNEY AHEAD

It's when ordinary people rise above the expectations and seize the opportunity that milestones truly are reached.
— Mike Huckabee

Reflecting on the Journey

As we reach the end of this guide, it's important to reflect on the journey you've embarked upon. Planning for your child's future is a profound and ongoing process involving countless decisions, sacrifices, and moments of pride. Every step taken, from early financial planning to teaching your child about the value of money, lays the groundwork for their future success.

Celebrating Milestones and Achievements

Throughout this journey, there will be many milestones to celebrate. These moments of achievement, whether it's saving enough for your child's education, seeing them start their own business, or witnessing their grand wedding, are testaments to your hard work and dedication. Celebrate these successes, no matter how big or small, as they are the fruits of your labor and love.

Embracing the Future with Confidence and Hope

The future is filled with uncertainties, but with a solid financial plan in place, you can embrace it with confidence and hope. Knowing that you've provided your child with the resources and knowledge they need to succeed can give you peace of mind. Encourage your child to dream big and pursue their passions, knowing they have a strong foundation to support them.

Final Thoughts and Encouragement

As parents, your role in your child's life is ongoing. Your support, guidance, and encouragement arc vital to their continued growth and success. Keep fostering an environment where your child feels valued and understood. Be their mentor, cheerleader, and advisor. Your involvement will continue to shape their path and help them navigate the challenges and opportunities that come their way.

Remember, the goal is to equip your child with the tools and confidence to face the future. Encourage them to explore endless possibilities and embrace opportunities with an open mind and heart. The journey may have its ups and downs, but with your unwavering support, your child can achieve great things.

As we conclude this guide, take pride in the steps you've taken and the plans you've made. Your commitment to your child's future is a powerful testament to your love and dedication. Here's to a future.

CHAPTER 10

UNDERSTANDING THE FINANCIAL ABUNDANCE PYRAMID

"The key to financial freedom and great wealth is a person's ability to convert earned income into passive and/or portfolio income."
– Robert Kiyosaki

1. **Starting with the Basics: Protection**

The first and most important part of the Financial Abundance Pyramid is **Starting with the Basics: Protection.** Think of this as the foundation of a house—everything else depends on it being strong and secure.

Protection is all about making sure that your family is safe financially, no matter what life throws at you.

This includes making sure your family is covered if something unexpected happens, like death, illness, disability or loss of income for any reason by means of the following instruments:

- **Life Insurance:** This is like a safety net. If something were to happen to you, life insurance would help your family financially, ensuring they can still pay bills, stay in their home, and continue with their lives without worrying about money.

- **Health Insurance:** Medical emergencies can be very expensive. Health insurance helps cover these costs so that you don't have to dip into your savings when someone in your family gets sick.

- **Disability Insurance:** If an accident or illness prevents you from working, disability insurance ensures that you still have an income to support your family.

- **Income Loss Coverage:** This is particularly important if you own a business or have a job that isn't guaranteed. It helps protect against financial hardship if your income suddenly stops.

By focusing on protection first, you're building a strong foundation that allows you to face the future with confidence, knowing your family is taken care of.

2. **Building a Safety Net: Secure and Steady Growth**

Once you've set up protection, the next step is **Building a Safety Net: Secure and Steady Growth.

This is about making sure that part of your money is safe and growing steadily without taking any big risks. It's like putting your money in a safe place where it can grow without being exposed to the ups and downs of the stock market or other risky investments.

This layer includes:

- **Savings Accounts or Fixed Deposits:** These are the safest places to put your money. They don't offer huge returns, but they are reliable and ensure that your money grows at a steady pace and stays forever.

- **Emergency Savings Fund:** It's important to have a fund that covers at least six months of living expenses. This money should be easily accessible in case you need it for emergencies, like if you lose your job or have unexpected expenses.

By ensuring that some of your money is growing in a safe, risk-free environment, you create a financial cushion that helps you weather any storms that might come your way.

3. **Aiming for More: Balanced Growth with a Little Risk**

   After you've secured the basics, you can start Aiming for More: Balanced Growth with a Little Risk.

   This step is about finding a balance between playing it safe and taking on some risk in order to grow your wealth faster. By now, you've already secured the money you need for emergencies and essential expenses, so you can afford to take a few calculated risks to increase your savings.

   In this stage, you might look into:

   - **Stocks and Mutual Funds:** These are investments that have the potential to grow your money more quickly than savings accounts, but they also come with some risk because the stock market can go up and down.

   - **Real Estate:** Buying property can be a good investment, as it often increases in value over time. However, it also comes with risks, like market fluctuations and maintenance costs.

   The key here is to balance the risk. Don't invest all your money in these options — just a portion that you can afford to take a chance on, knowing that you have your safety net already in place.

4. Reaching for the Stars: High-Growth Opportunities

At the top of the pyramid is ''Reaching for the Stars: High-Growth Opportunities''.

This part is for those who are willing to take bigger risks in the hope of getting bigger rewards. However, it's important to be cautious because these investments can be unpredictable.

High-growth investments might include:

- **Aggressive Stocks or Venture Capital:** These are investments that have the potential to bring in high returns, but they are also much riskier. The value can go up quickly, but it can also drop just as fast.

- **Startups or New Business Ventures:** Investing in a new business can be exciting and profitable, but it's also risky because there's no guarantee the business will succeed.

While it's tempting to put a lot of money into high-growth opportunities, it's important to remember the saying, "Don't put all your eggs in one basket."

Only a small portion of your money should be in this category, and you should be prepared for the possibility of losing it.

5. The Red Zone: Avoiding the Gamble of Speculation

At the very top of the pyramid, and something you should generally avoid, is **The Red Zone: Avoiding the Gamble of Speculation.** Speculation is essentially gambling with your money. It involves making very high-risk investments with the hope of making a quick profit, but it often leads to big losses.

Speculative investments include:

- **Day Trading:** Buying and selling stocks rapidly in hopes of making quick profits. This is highly risky and can result in significant financial loss.

- **Cryptocurrencies or Unproven Ventures:** These can be extremely volatile and are not recommended as part of a stable financial plan, especially when planning for a child's future.

Speculation is not a good strategy when you're planning for important goals like your child's education or your family's long-term financial security. It's better to stick with safer, more reliable investment strategies that are less likely to result in financial loss.

To Sum it Up

The Financial Abundance Pyramid is a practical and structured approach to managing your finances in a way that protects your family, ensures steady growth, and allows for future prosperity.

By starting with a solid foundation of protection, securing a safety net, and then cautiously taking on more risk as you move up the pyramid, you can create a financial plan that not only supports your family's present needs but also paves the way for a secure and abundant future.

Remember, the goal is to build a strong, stable financial structure that can withstand any challenges while still offering opportunities for growth.

By following this pyramid, you can ensure that your family is financially protected, your money grows steadily, and you have the potential for future wealth—all without taking unnecessary risks.

Now is the time to take action!

- Start by evaluating your current financial situation.

- Do you have the proper protections in place for your family?

- Are you growing your savings safely and steadily?

- What steps can you take to start building for the future?

By following the Financial Abundance Pyramid, you can create a secure and prosperous future for your family.

Take the first step today— Book a 1-2-1 session to create a roadmap which will protect your family, and begin your journey toward financial abundance.

Your child's future depends on the decisions you make now. Let's ensure that their future is bright, secure, and filled with opportunities!

Money Vikas Financial Services

Address: 714,7th Floor, Aggarwal Millennium Tower-1,
        Netaji Subhash Place, Pitampura, New Delhi- 110034

Contact: 9560058586, 011-47553805, 8527200308